PuzzleMania®
Halloween Puzzles

HIGHLIGHTS PRESS
Honesdale, Pennsylvania

CONTENTS

When you finish a puzzle, check it off √.
Good luck, and happy puzzling!

A-Mazing!

Poetry Break

Hidden Pictures®

Do the Math

Secret Codes

Look Twice

Wordplay

Crafts, Jokes & Games

Tic Tac Row

Each of these trick-or-treaters has something in common with the other trick-or-treaters in the same row. For example, in the first row across all three trick-or-treaters are wearing green. Look at the other rows across, down, and diagonally. Can you tell what's alike in each row?

Match-o'-Lanterns

Pete Peterson's Pumpkin Emporium is famous for its jack-o'-lanterns. This year, Pete has added a new twist. Every jack-o'-lantern has one that matches it exactly. Can you find all the matching pairs?

Illustrated by Garry Colby

Bat-ting Order

More than 900 kinds of bats live in the world. Thirty-five are hiding in this grid. How many can you find? Look up, down, across, backwards, and diagonally. When you're done, search the leftover letters for more bats. If you can find all **13** extra **BAT**s, you've got a perfect batting average.

Word List

BIG-EARED

BONNETED

BROWN

BUMBLEBEE

CAVE

COLONIAL

DAWN

EASTERN RED

EVENING

FREE-TAILED

FRINGED

GHOST-FACED

GOLDEN

GRAY

HOARY

HORSESHOE

INDIANA

KEEN'S

LEAF-NOSED

LONG-EARED

LONG-NOSED

MASTIFF

NECTAR

PALLID

SMALL-FOOTED

SMOKY

SOUTHEASTERN

SOUTHERN YELLOW

SPOTTED

TRI-COLORED

VAMPIRE

VESPER

WESTERN RED

WOOLLY

WRINKLE-FACED

```
L O N G N O S E D A B A T Q X R B
B A T W S M A L L F O O T E D E A
I N D I A N A (B I G E A R E D) P T
S C I L T D A R N D E T T O P S E
O C O L O N I A L B A T N S A E O H
U T R I C O L O R E D R T B A V E
T A G H O S T F A C E D A S B D S
H V A M P I R E A T E T T A E B E
E T N B A T T S S L W E N T A D S
R K E E N S M A I B R T E T A E R
N Y D A T O E A A N I N C A P R O
Y B L A K H T T R B N B T T A A H
E A O Y T E B E A O K T A F L E W
L T G U E A D T B T L G R F L G O
L G O R G N I N E V E R A I I N O
O S F B B A T E C H F A B T D O L
W E S T E R N R E D A Y A S C L L
L E A F N O S E D B C Y R A O H Y
B U M B L E B E E A E B V M B A T
B D F R I N G E D T D E B R O W N
```

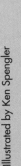

9

Illustrated by Ken Spengler

Monster Maze

The Frankenstein family has the best Halloween candy on the block. Be sure to stop by their house on your way home. Do not cross a path with a bat on it.

Once you go from Start to Finish, write the letters from the correct path in order in the spaces to answer the riddle.

What is a werewolf's favorite book?

_____ _____ _____ _____ _____ _____ _____ _____ _____ _____

11

Hidden Pictures®
Haunted House

slice of orange

bowl

ax

pennant

tack

crown

crayon

paintbrush

fishhook

golf club

toothbrush

snow cone

drinking straw

snake

lollipop

mushroom

spoon

heart

slice of pie

nail

comb

ice-cream bar

sailboat

Illustrated by Olivia Cole

Halloween Jig

By Leland B. Jacobs
Illustrated by Dan McGeehan

There was a little goblin
who, on one Halloween,
took his little piccolo
out to the village green.
He played a tune so sweetly,
he played with such delight,
that ghosts came out from shadows
and danced in robes of white.
And several little monsters,
who rarely came in view,
jigged and jumped and hopped about
as only monsters do.
The little goblin's playing
there on the village green
gave all those ghosts and monsters
a treat for Halloween.

BOO!

At the Puzzlemania Costume Shop, the costumes are more than just fun—they're also code crackers! Use this list of costumes to solve this puzzle.

Each coded space has two numbers. The first number tells you which spot to look at; the second number tells you which letter in that item to use. For example, the first coded letter is 2-2. The first 2 tells you to go to CLOWN. Count 2 letters in, and you've got an L. Fill in the rest to scare up the answers to these Halloween jokes.

Costume List

1. **GHOST**
2. **CLOWN**
3. **PIRATE**
4. **KNIGHT**
5. **COWBOY**
6. **LADYBUG**
7. **MONSTER**
8. **PRINCESS**
9. **TYRANNOSAURUS REX**

Hidden Pictures

Hidden in the

There is more than meets the eye at this pumpkin farm. Can you find the hidden objects?

Illustrated by Kevin Rechin

Pumpkin Patch

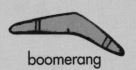

boomerang

pennant

ring

rake

fishhook

umbrella

canoe

paper clip

open book

slice of pie

feather

comb

envelope

key

mitten

megaphone

fish

ruler

kite

football

crown

mug

banana

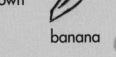

17

Spooky Search

Twenty words to do with Halloween are lurking in this jack-o'-lantern. They are hiding up, down, across, backwards, and diagonally. Don't be scared to jump right in!

Word List

~~BATS~~	HAUNTED HOUSE	PARTY
BLACK CAT	HAYRIDE	PUMPKIN
CANDY	MASK	SPIDER
CIDER	MOON	SPOOKY
CORN	NIGHT	TREAT
COSTUME	OCTOBER	TRICK
GHOST	PARADE	

```
              P     T
              P     A
      B  V  A  N  C  R  Y  A
      O  A  R  B  I  A  B  A  J  P
   O  V  Y  E  O  G  N  C  I  D  E  R
   O  T  Y  S  O  H  D  O  W  E  C  B
G  E  R  P        T  Y        B  O  Y  Q
H  M  I  H  A  Y  R  I  D  E  B  O  O  R  K  B
O  U  C  T  A  C  K  C  A  L  B  O  O  N  O  O
S  T  K        S  P  I  D  E  R     B  O  O
T  S  R  B                       N  O  P  K
O  O  B  E  O                 X  O  O  S  T
C  O  O  A  O  R  E  B  O  T  C  O  A  R
B  O  O  O  O  T  R  A  N  I  K  P  M  U  P
H  A  U  N  T  E  D  H  O  U  S  E
```

Bonus Puzzle

Can you find the word **BOO** 13 times in the grid?

18

Box Out!

Follow the directions to cross out certain boxes. When you're done, write the remaining letters in order from left to right and top to bottom. They will give you the answer to the riddle.

Cross out all numbers divisible by 3.
Cross out all numbers divisible by 8.

M ~~8~~	T 13	Y 40	N 24	H 17	A 12
O 15	M 16	C 33	E 20	C 18	A 30
L 32	E 25	F 48	T 36	L 10	O 64
R 45	F 28	D 3	R 66	A 26	Y 42
Z 56	E 21	B 38	B 72	T 80	W 54
E 22	K 39	N 51	H 6	T 44	S 27

What do magical creatures learn in school?

__ __ __   __ __ __ \- __ __ __ __

Mansion of Mystery

Many treasure hunters have tried to spend a night in the spooky old King mansion, searching for its vast hidden fortune. Starting at the front door, follow the directions and gather the letters in the proper sequence. These will lead you to the treasure and will tell you what is hidden in the locked trunk.

1. Before going in, take the letter from the door knocker. Now look for the grandfather clock.
2. Take the letter from the clock. Head upstairs to the red room.
3. You want the letter on the pillow. Now get something to eat.
4. Open the refrigerator slowly for the next letter. Head into the garden.
5. The letter you're after is growing from that mound. Go up the kitchen stairs.
6. Along the way, pull the letter from the second painting.
7. Go to the attic, where the spiders have the letter you want.
8. Outside on the roof is where the next letter is shining. Be careful!
9. Back inside, the library has the next letter you need. Take the yellow one.
10. As you pull that letter, a secret panel swings open to reveal the treasure. Look straight in to find the last letter.
11. To uncover what's in the waiting chest, take the letters you've collected and read them backwards.

Illustrated by
Liisa Chauncy

20

21

Craft a Haunted-House Party

Invite neighborhood ghosties and ghoulies to the spookiest celebration in town! Try the eerie ideas here, and create your own ghostly host: Wear a costume cut from a white bedsheet and decorated with markers. You might also serve phantom foods such as popcorn, white (no-sauce) English-muffin pizzas, and vanilla cupcakes.

Spooky Invitation

1 Fold a sheet of **construction paper** in half, then in half again. On the front, draw a house with windows and doors. Cut around three sides of each window and the door so they open and close.

2 Glue **light-colored paper** behind the front. Be careful not to glue the windows and door shut.

3 Open up the windows and door, and draw pictures of whatever is haunting the house! Inside the card, write out the date, time, and other details of your party.

Eerie Bookmark Party Favor

1 Cut out ghost and bat shapes from **paper**.

2 Add details with **markers**.

3 Tape a long piece of **yarn** or a **chenille stick** onto the back.

Haunted Lantern

1 Use **markers** to draw and color a house on the front of a paper bag.

2 Cut out the windows and doors.

3 Place a **flashlight** inside the bag to cast an eerie glow. Use this as a table centerpiece, or make a few lanterns that lead to your front door.

Napkin Goblin

1 Cut a 2-inch-wide section from each side of a clean **plastic food container** or a **large plastic cup**, leaving the bottom intact.

2 Decorate the outside of the container as you like.

3 Place paper napkins in the cutout section.

Boo-tiful Place Marker

1 For each place marker, cut a ghost shape and a 3-inch circle from a clean **white plastic-foam tray**.

2 Cut the circle in half. Cut two slits in the bottom of the ghost and one into the curved top of each half-circle.

3 Fit the half-circle slits into the bottom slits so the ghost stands upright.

4 Add **cut-paper** eyes, a mouth, and a pumpkin with a **chenille-stick** handle. Twist **tissue paper** into a bow tie. Write the name of each guest on a ghost.

Floating Ghost

1 Cut out two arms from **white paper**. Glue them to the sides of a **white paper bag**.

2 Use **markers** to draw a face.

3 Stuff the bag with **newspaper** and staple it closed. Tie **clear fishing line** on top as an "invisible" hanger.

Photo of boy by Ken Karp

23

Funny Farm

How many silly things can you find in this picture?

The Pumpkin Patch

OPEN

UP ALL Night

This page is crawling with animals that are awake at night. We've gathered **21** kinds of nocturnal animals. Their names fit into the grid in just one way. Use the number of letters in each word as a clue to where it might fit.

3 Letters
BAT
EEL
OWL
RAT

5 Letters
KOALA
SKUNK

6 Letters
BADGER
WOMBAT

7 Letters
CATFISH
HAMSTER
LEOPARD
OPOSSUM
RACCOON

8 Letters
HEDGEHOG
PLATYPUS
SCORPION

9 Letters
ARMADILLO
CROCODILE
TARANTULA

11 Letters
BAT-EARED FOX
NIGHT MONKEY

E E L

Wendy Witch's Stew

ring

ice-cream
bar

snowman

candle

ladder

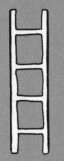
present

slice of bread

pencil

ice-cream cone

mitten

truck

teacup

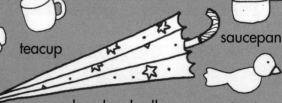
closed umbrella

saucepan

bird

26

A Total Hoot

Look closely to find all the pairs of numbers next to each other that add up to **20**. These pairs may go across, down, or diagonally. Every number will be used as part of one pair.

12	17	3	14	7	16	4
1	8	15	6	13	10	3
19	10	10	5	10	17	12
16	2	9	11	19	8	18
4	7	18	6	1	9	2
13	0	20	14	15	5	11

Crafts

Wall-Shadow Cat

1 Draw a cat shape on **tracing paper**.

2 Hold the paper against a window with the cat facing outside, so the light helps the design show through. Trace around the design with a **glue stick**. Set aside until almost dry but still slightly tacky.

3 Cut a sheet from a **plastic trash bag**, and press it onto the glued side of the paper. Turn it over and cut through along the shape's outline.

4 Peel off the plastic shadow. Rub it against your hair or clothes, then press it onto a wall. The shadow will stay up for days! Try a pumpkin face, too.

Handy Spider

1 Paint two **styrofoam balls** (one bigger than the other) black. To join the balls, put glue on each end of a **craft stick**. Insert one end into each ball.

2 For legs, insert three **black chenille sticks** into each side of the body. Glue a **black pompom** to the end of each leg. For arms, insert two **black chenille sticks** into the front of the body. Cut four hands from **black felt**, and glue two hands around the end of each arm.

3 For a face, glue on **pompoms** and cut-**felt** features.

Bat Spinner

1 Fold a **black chenille stick** around a **drinking straw**, making a loop. Twist the ends together to keep the stick in place.

2 Wrap **electrical tape** above and below the chenille-stick loop on the straw.

3 Cut out a bat shape from **black construction paper**. Decorate the bat with a **silver marker**. Tape the bat to the ends of the chenille stick

4 Make your bat "fly" by holding the straw's end and spinning your wrist.

WHO'S THERE?

There are three knock-knock jokes on this page. It's up to you to crack the code and fill in the jokes. Each number stands for a different letter. Once you know one number's letter, you can fill in that letter in all of the jokes. So, what are you waiting for? Someone's at the door!

1

$\underset{1}{K}\ \underset{2}{N}\ \underset{3}{O}\ \underset{4}{C}\ \underset{1}{K}\ \ \underset{1}{K}\ \underset{2}{N}\ \underset{3}{O}\ \underset{4}{C}\ \underset{1}{K}$,

5 6 3 7   8 6 9 10 9 ?

17 3 10 11 7 .

17 3 10 11 7   5 6 3 ?

17 3 10 11 7   14 3 4 1 9 17 ,

8 6 12 8 7   5 6 20 11

6 12 17 8 3   1 2 3 4 1 .

2

1 2 3 4 1   1 2 3 4 1 ,

5 6 3 7   8 6 9 10 9 ?

7 12 17 11 9 .

7 12 17 11 9   5 6 3 ?

7 12 17 11 9   18 12 19 11 4 ,

5 3 10 17 7   12 2 17   11 14 14

8 9 14 14   20 3 15 .

3

1 2 3 4 1   1 2 3 4 1 ,

5 6 3 7   8 6 9 10 9 ?

2 3 12 6 .

2 3 12 6   5 6 3 ?

2 3 12 6   19 3 3 17

21 14 12 4 9   8 3 16 11 2 17

18 3 10 9   22 3 1 9 7 ?

Who?

29

Castle Calculation

People say there is a secret treasure hidden inside this creepy castle. To find it, you must be a quick thinker as well as a quick runner. Each time you pass one of the wall torches, the secret door either locks or unlocks itself. For example, if you pass a torch and the door

START

unlocks, the very next time you pass a torch, the door will relock itself. You cannot go back over your path or the door will seal itself for another hundred years. The door is now locked. Can you find a path that will bring you into the library while the secret door is open?

Illustrated by Jerry Zimmerman

Hidden Pictures® Open House

artist's brush

wishbone

golf club

crescent moon

fish

eyeglasses

clothespin

pliers

snake

safety pin

sock

spoon

Illustrated by R. Michael Palan

Scrambled Bugs

Don't let this page bug you! Just unscramble these insect names. Once you've got them straightened out, put the numbered letters in the correct spaces. This will give you the answer to the riddle.

TAN ○○○
    2

THOM ○○○○
     4

LEAF ○○○○
    7

PAWS ○○○○
  6

KICT ○○○○
  3

TANG ○○○○
     11

LEETEB ○○○○○○
    12

DEBUBG ○○○○○○
 8

KITCREC ○○○○○○○
   10

SOOTQUIM ○○○○○○○○
    5

GANDRYFLO ○○○○○○○○○
      1

GRAPHPOSERS ○○○○○○○○○○○
      9

Where does a spider keep its photos?

○ N ○ ○○ ○○ ○○ ○ ○○
1 2 3 4 5 6 7 8 9 10 11 12

33

Monster Mash

It's time for the annual Horrible Hoedown at Castle Karloff. As an added party favor, our host has posted this coded riddle. Use the key to figure out what each symbol means and to decipher the secret message.

Why do grave diggers make excellent storytellers?

Laboratory Labyrinth

Dr. Zarkoff is up to his old tricks. To add the final ingredient to his energy shake, he's dropping this grape into the beaker. See if you can follow the tubes around to let the doctor know where the grape will end up. Hint: In Dr. Zarkoff's maze, a funnel will catch any grape dropped into it, and the grape will then continue on.

ENERGY SHAKE

Goody Game

Go trick-or-treating around the neighborhood without leaving your house. This board game is great to play at your Halloween party. After everyone has crossed the finish line, you can all munch on your candy-corn "winnings!"

What You Need

- **Pinking shears**
- **Poster board**
- **Paper plate**
- **Metal fastener**
- **Markers**
- **Candy corn or other treats**

What to Do

1 Using pinking shears, cut out a circle of poster board that is slightly larger than the underside of the plate. Color the edge of the circle orange.

2 Divide the circle into eight even wedges. Draw and color a house in each of the sections. Write game directions under each of the houses, such as:

- **Jackpot! Get 5 candies. Move 3 spaces.**
- **Bag ripped. Lose 2 candies. Move 5 spaces.**
- **Getting late. Jump ahead 2 spaces. Spin again.**
- **Share a candy from the pot with everyone.**
- **Flashlight failed. Go to START. Spin again.**
- **Bellyache. Give everyone 1 piece of your candy. Move 4 spaces.**
- **Get 2 candies. Move 2 spaces.**
- **Get 1 candy. Spin again.**

3 Turn the plate upside down. With a metal fastener, attach the circle to the center.

4 Make sixteen "sidewalk" spaces on the plate's edge, as shown. Label one line START and FINISH. Draw an arrow in the center of each space, pointing toward the spinner.

5 Cut out and decorate small circles of poster board for game markers.

To Play: Place the trick-or-treater markers on the sidewalk at the START. Take turns moving and collecting candy corn according to what you spin.

38

Tic Tac Row

Each of these castles has something in common with the other two castles in the same row. For example, in the first row across all three castles are white. Look at the other rows across, down, and diagonally. Can you tell what's alike in each row?

  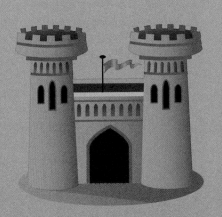

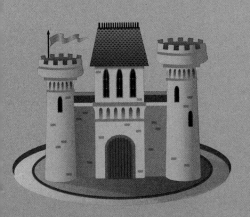  

Illustrated by Tim Davis

Crafts

Crafts That Go Boo!

Spooky-Creature Walking Game

By Annie Beer

1. For each character game piece, cut two cups from a **cardboard egg carton**. Glue the cups together. Let them dry completely. Make five game pieces.
2. Using **acrylic paint**, decorate the game pieces to look like a cat, a ghost, a mummy, a bat, and a pumpkin.
3. For the house, decorate an empty **tissue box** with paint, **markers**, and **colored paper**.

To Play: Play the game in a large room. The object of the game is to move around the edge of the room; whoever makes it back to the starting point first wins.

Place the characters in the house. Assign one player to be in charge of pulling a character from the house on each player's turn. The character he or she selects represents the number of steps that player will take.

Cat: Leap forward 3 large steps.
Mummy: Walk backward 2 large steps.
Bat: Hop forward 2 small steps.
Ghost: Glide forward 2 normal steps.
Pumpkin: Stay still.

Garland for Autumn

By Rachael Decker

1. Cut circles out of **poster board**.
2. Draw the outline of a fruit or vegetable on each circle.
3. Crumple bits of **tissue paper**. Glue them within the outlines. Add **construction-paper** details.
4. Punch a hole in the top of each circle. Tie the circles together using **raffia** or **yarn**.

Pumpkin-Patch Pals

This spirited trio will add spice to your Halloween decorating.

1. Cut six cups from the egg carton. Glue them together in pairs to make three pumpkins. Paint them orange.
2. Cut a section of three peaks from the egg carton for the base. Trim two peaks different heights. Paint the base black.
3. Glue the pumpkins to the base. Attach cut-paper features to the pumpkins. Place your jack-o'-lanterns on a windowsill or table.

More Ideas

Make lots of egg-carton jack-o'-lanterns, without the base, and hand them out with candy to trick-or-treaters.

You Will Need:
- cardboard egg carton
- paint
- construction paper

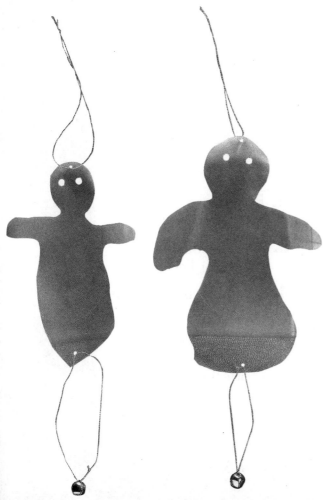

Jingle Ghosts

Are those ghosts ringing?

1. Cut ghost shapes from the sides of the milk jug.
2. Punch eyeholes in the head of each ghost.
3. Poke a small hole in the top of each ghost. Tie a loop of thread through each hole to make a hanger. Poke a small hole in the bottom of each ghost. Thread a jingle bell onto a piece of thread, and tie the thread to the ghost.

More Ideas

Hang the ghosts in a breezy place to hear the bells jingle.

You Will Need:
- plastic milk jug
- hole punch
- thread
- jingle bells

Haunted Logic

Trevor and four of his friends went to a Halloween party. Using the clues below, can you figure out what costume each friend wore and what treat each brought to share?

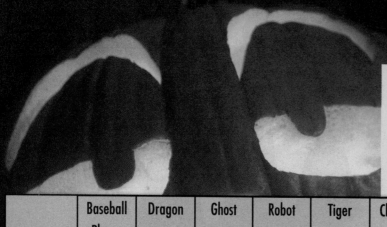

Use the chart to keep track of your answers. Put an **X** in each box that can't be true and an **O** in boxes that match.

	Baseball Player	Dragon	Ghost	Robot	Tiger	Chocolate Bars	Gum	Licorice	Raisins	Taffy
Trevor										
Rachel										
Eli										
Annie										
Troy										

1. One boy's costume and treat start with the same letter as his name.

2. Eli dressed as his idol, Babe Ruth.

3. Rachel does not like robots or licorice.

4. Trevor brought a treat made from grapes.

5. Annie brought the treat with the shortest name, but her costume's name was longer than three others.

M Is for Monsters

At least thirty objects in this picture
begin with the letter M. How many can you find?

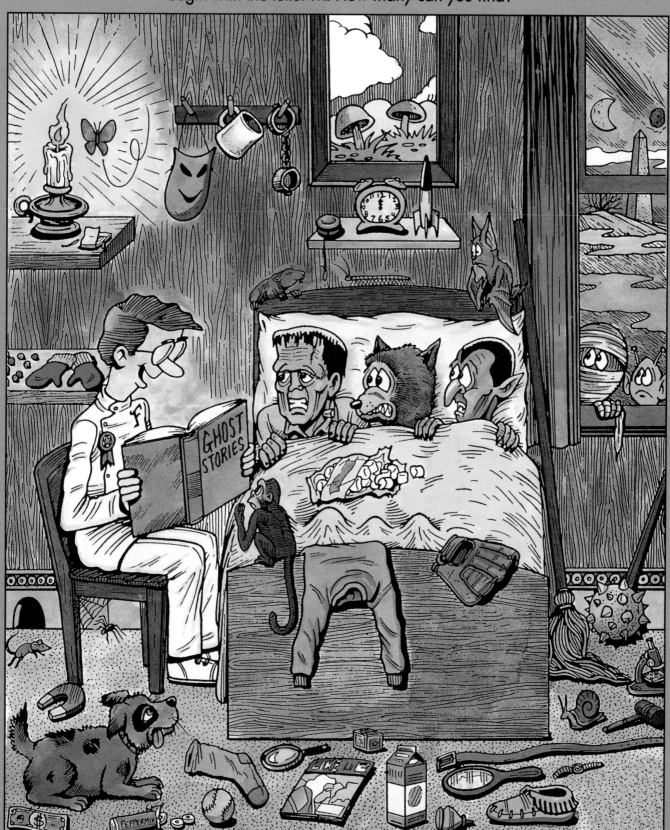

Illustrated by Joe Seidita

Party Time

This party has a prize for the best costume. Before the judging begins, see if you can uncover at least **20** differences between these pictures.

One of these masks does NOT appear on this page. Which one?

45

Going Batty

Lead Dr. Livingstone through this labyrinth of winged things back to the cave entrance.

finish

start

Hidden Pictures®
Spooky Sale

Pumpkins and Apples for Sale

banana

drinking straw

crayon

shovel

needle

doughnut

heart

fish

teacup

light bulb

musical note

screw

ring

crescent moon

ice-cream cone

47

Puzzling Pirates

Four great pirates once sailed the seven seas. They left behind some cryptic clues for any hardy soul brave enough to search for their treasures. Cut through the clues to find each pirate's treasure, where it was hidden, what it was buried in, and the name of that pirate's ship.

Use the grid to keep track of your answers. Put a circle in a box where the information matches according to the clues. Put an X in a box where the information doesn't match. For example, clue 1 says Orangebeard was not the captain of the Leaking Lena. So we've already put an X in the box where the Orangebeard row meets the Leaking Lena column.

Take your time with this very tricky puzzle. It's already stumped fifteen men. Yo-ho-ho!

CLUES

1. Orangebeard, who was not the captain of the Leaking Lena, had never sailed to any island that began with an H.

2. Whitebeard never liked silver or jewels, and he would never give his ship a happy name.

3. The Ocean Queen had a full cargo of baseball cards when it docked in Tahiti.

4. Purplebeard was the only pirate ever seen in the backyard, and he was carrying a jar of jewels.

5. Blackbeard's ship was not named after a bird, and the place where he buried his bag of booty has the most vowels in it.

6. The metal box contains the baseball cards.

	Haiti	Tahiti	Hawaii	Backyard	Chest	Jar	Metal Box	Bag	Gold	Silver	Jewels	Baseball Cards	Jolly Roger	Smiling Sea Gull	Leaking Lena	Ocean Queen
Blackbeard																
Orangebeard														X		
Whitebeard																
Purplebeard																
Jolly Roger																
Smiling Sea Gull																
Leaking Lena																
Ocean Queen																
Gold																
Silver																
Jewels																
Baseball Cards																
Chest																
Jar																
Metal Box																
Bag																

Illustrated by Scott Peck

SUPER CHALLENGE

Only one of the pirates in this puzzle is the namesake of a real buccaneer. Can you tell who is the credible captain?

49

Candy Counter

No need to sugarcoat it, this is a sweet puzzle! Each of these candy names will fit into the grid in just one way. Use a word's length as a clue for where to put it. When you've filled them all in, write the letters in the shaded boxes in order in the spaces below to see the answer to the riddle.

What crop does a farmer with a sweet tooth grow?

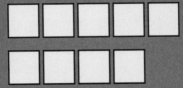

Tic Tac Row

Each of these scarecrows has something in common with the two others in the same row. For example, all three scarecrows in the top row across are wearing red hats. Look at the other rows across, down, and diagonally. What's alike in each row?

Illustrated by John Nez

A Squeaky House

There's a mouse in the house! More than one, if you know where to look. There are **20** mice hidden in the scene. How many can you find?

Illustrated by Kevin Rechin

Minus Maze

At the entrance of this maze, you have 25 points. You can exit only if you have exactly 0 points when you reach the orange arrow. Go through the maze subtracting the amount you have to give the goblins as you pass them. Hint: The first two numbers you'll come to are 3 and 6.

Illustrated by David Justice

Three Ghostesses

Three little ghostesses,
Sitting on postesses,
Eating buttered toastesses,
Greasing up their fistesses,
Up to their wristesses,
Oh, what beastesses
To make such feastesses!

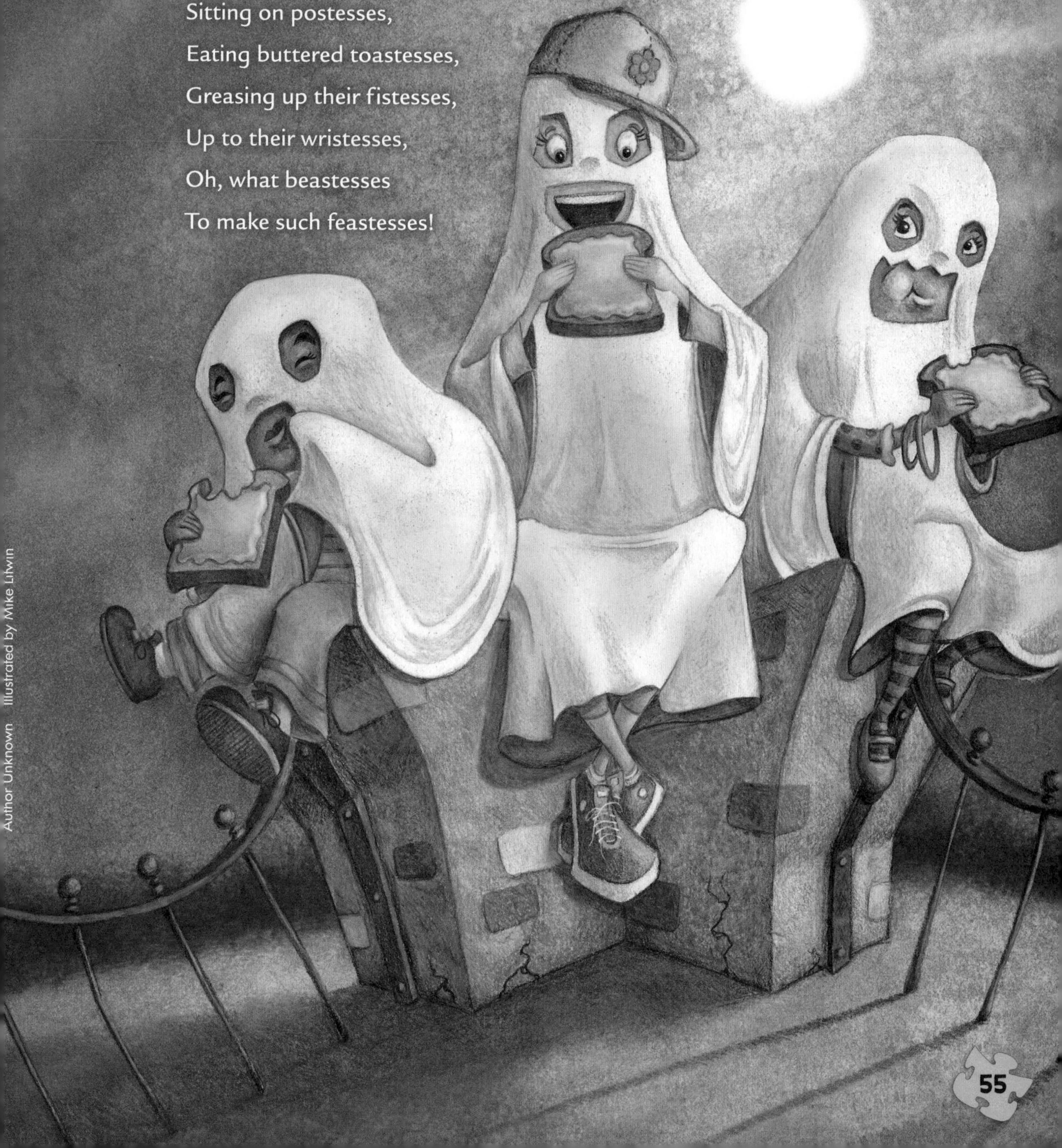

Author Unknown   Illustrated by Mike Litwin

Monster Party

narla, Growlie, and Mo are picking up their costumes for the big party!
ollow the paths to see who gets which one.

Halloween Parade

Can you find the hidden objects below?
When you finish, you can color in the rest of the scene.

pencil

nail

tree

bow

snake

comb

teacup

drinking glass

bowl

candle

sailboat

Snooperstition

It might be bad luck to do this puzzle while stepping on a banana peel.
But it might be good luck to do this puzzle while thinking of a hippopotamus.
Superstitions are signs that people believe have to do with luck. Try to find all
the symbols of good or bad luck in this picture. Good luck!

Illustrated by Leslie Harris

Bat Speak

A winged thing brings this secret messaging system from El Salvador.

Which mammal flies at night and has a secret code of its own? If you lived in the Central American country of El Salvador, you'd know the answer: a bat.

In Spanish, the word for bat is *murciélago* (moor-see-AY-lah-go). Salvadoran children write messages to each other in a code that they also call *murciélago*.

Try It!

Substitute a number for each letter of *murciélago*.

1	2	3	4	5	6	7	8	9	0
M	**U**	**R**	**C**	**I**	**E**	**L**	**A**	**G**	**O**

Write a word using numbers instead of letters. For instance, if your name were **Maria**, your code name would be **18358**.

For letters that aren't in the word *murciélago*, simply use the regular letters. For example, there is no *s* in *murciélago*, so if your name were **Carlos**, your code name would be **48370S**.

Translate your name and other words into *murciélago* code. With a little practice, you'll be ready to write longer coded messages to your friends.

H8PPY 40D5N9!

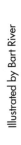

Illustrated by Bart River

Code Challenge!

Notice that *murciélago* contains many letters (10), all the vowels (A, E, I, O, U), and no repeated consonants (M, R, C, L, G). Try to think of a similar word in English, then create a code of your own.

Leaves and Bounds

Hidden Pictures

There is more than meets the eye in this backyard. Can you find the hidden objects?

 kite

 book

 T-shirt

 hockey stick

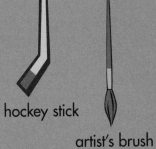 artist's brush

 banana

 ruler

 saw

 mitten

 light bulb

 paper clip

 slice of bread

 duck

 snail

 spoon

 cane

 bugle

 fishhook

 peanut

 shovel

top hat

 ice-cream cone

 fish

 **63**

Whose Home?

The library volunteers are walking each trick-or-treater home after listening to Halloween stories. Working with the directions from the boys and girls,

Pam: "I'll go south two blocks and make a left. At the next corner, I'll make a right. My house is on this block."

Meredith: "To get to my house, I go east to the first right. Then I go two blocks south. Next I head east again for one block. My house is on this corner."

Donald: "I'll walk Quinn home first. Then I'll go back southwest to the corner. From there, I'll head northwest and then make a slight turn left to the second block. One more right and I walk to the second house."

Frank: "I like to walk around town before going home. I usually go south three blocks, then east one. I head north for one block and then east again. At the second corner, I turn left. At the next corner, I turn left again. I make the next right and head north. A sharp turn east at the next corner and you're at my house."

Gary: "I'll walk Meredith home first. Then I'll head north one block before turning west and going to the last house on the map."

Quinn: "I go south from the library to the first corner. Then I turn left. At the next corner, I go south again and then left again. Then I turn right to the bridge. At the end of this road I have to go a short way northeast to reach my house."

Wendy: "I like to see the cows, so I walk east first. At the third right, I turn southwest and walk to the corner. I wait here a while before moving south. At the next corner, I turn right. At the third right, I make a left. When I can't go anymore, I turn east. The first house I come to is mine."

can you help each person find the right house, starting from the library? Each child's name begins with the same initial letter as his or her costume.

Mummy Maze

Morton the Mummy has forgotten the secret passage to his royal chamber. Can you help him find his way back?

FINISH

Illustrated by Gregg Valley

Kooky Spooks

How many differences can you find between these two pictures?

Illustrated by Bill Basso

Hidden Pictures®
Carving Jack-o'-Lanterns

sailboat

crown

ice-cream cone

shoe

birdhouse

turtle

artist's brush

Illustrated by Olivia Cole

bird

ax

tack

question mark

flag

butterfly

mouse

handbell

fish

mushroom

jar

crescent moon

candle

cupcake

Create a Goody Bag

Tote your treats home in style!

Snack Pack

1   Cut off the two long top flaps of a **large cereal box**. Fold in and glue the two small top flaps to the inside of the cereal box. These will be reinforcements for the handle.

2   Cut a **half-gallon milk carton** in half. Glue **black construction paper** over the carton and the box. Glue the two containers together.

3   Cut out ghosts from **white paper**. Glue to the tote box. Add **yarn** along the top.

4   Poke a small hole on each narrow side of the box. Thread yarn through the holes from the outside of the box, and tie the yarn into knots on the inside.

Shiny Sack

1   Fold over the top of a **brown-paper bag** several times to make a cuff. Decorate the bag with a jack-o'-lantern cut from **aluminum foil**. Add **foam-paper** features. Glue a strip of foil to the top.

2   For the handle, cut three pieces of **yarn** the same length. Knot the pieces together about 1 inch from one end. Braid by folding A over B and then C over A. Continue until the yarn is braided. Tie the ends into a knot about 1 inch from the other end.

3   Staple the handle ends to the sides of the bag.

Adventures in the Night

This house looks friendly, but in the cellar
Lurks a mean and nasty feller
Who plans to ruin Halloween
For every child, adult, and teen.
When trick-or-treaters all feel dandy,
He'll jump out to grab their candy.
But now the kids can spoil his plan
If only they can cross the land.
To help catch this creep, simply say
What objects they'll find along the way:
Apple, candle, spider, hat,
Jack-o'-lantern, then a cat,
An owl, a crown, broom, and bat.
Once confronted, the sneak will scat,
The candy's recovered and that's that.

START

70

HAPPY HALLOWEEN

FINISH

Illustrated by Charles Jordan

72

PARTY SEARCH

Can you find?

Can you also find four bats in this picture?

Illustrated by Scott Burroughs

FIRE CHIEF

73

Don't Be Afraid...

The words in this list are associated with October 31. First find and circle all of them in the grid, either across, up, down, backward, or diagonally. Then darken in all the letters found in HALLOWEEN that were not part of any word you circled. When done correctly, a picture will appear.

BAG
BATS
BLACK
BOO
BREW
BROOMS
CANDY
CATS
COSTUMES
CREEPY
FUN
GHOSTS
GHOULS
GOBLINS
GOOD
HALLOWEEN
HAT
HOWL
MASK
MONSTERS
MOON
NIGHT
ORANGE
PUMPKINS
SCARY
SCREAM
TRICK OR TREAT
WITCHES
WOLF

```
B G O T R I C K O R T R E A T
G H O U L S E M U T S O C C J
G O B L I N S U A J W O L F K
O S C A R Y I L Z Y P E E R C
O T B N E W T O R H L A R G A
D S L V B C O L W U D X E B L
S H C A N D Y M A E R C S E B
N W G E O M A S K L E F M E S
I A S G N E T Y W E L T O A R
K O T N E E W O L L A H O O E
P L A A E I H A P H N G R L T
M E B R C L F U N H Z I B H S
U T O O C N W A L H V N E J N
P B C L S E H C T I W E M C O
P S T A C H A N H A E N N O O M
```

Illustrated by Tom Powers

74

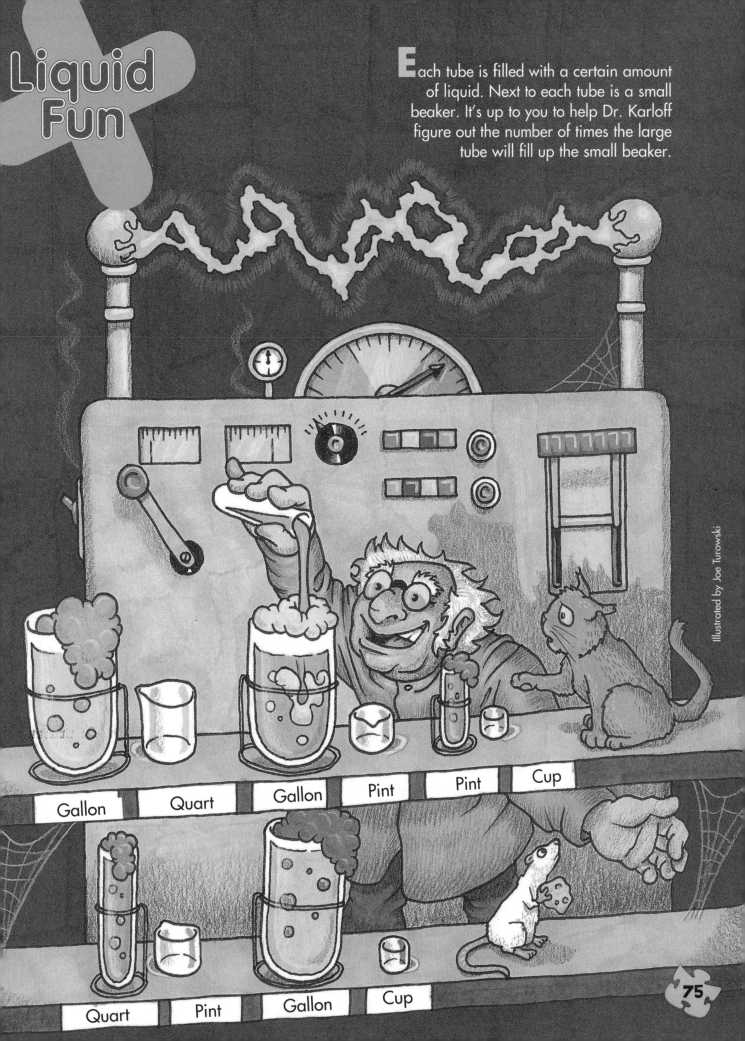

Liquid Fun

Each tube is filled with a certain amount of liquid. Next to each tube is a small beaker. It's up to you to help Dr. Karloff figure out the number of times the large tube will fill up the small beaker.

Gallon   Quart   Gallon   Pint   Pint   Cup

Quart   Pint   Gallon   Cup

Illustrated by Joe Turowski

Trick or Treat?

ck and Rita collected candy on Halloween. Find the path home for each of them.
ount the candies on the path. Who got more?

FINISH

FINISH

Illustrated by Sean Parkes

77

Imagine That!

This puzzle is crawling—and flying and trotting and swimming—with creatures straight out of fantasy worlds. Can you catch them all? Each will fit into the grid in only one way. Use the size of each word as a clue to where it might fit. We have filled in one to get you started. If you can fill the entire grid, you're a legend in the making!

Word List

3 letters
ELF
ROC

4 letters
OGRE

5 letters
FAIRY
GENIE
GIANT
GNOME
PIXIE
TROLL

6 letters
DRAGON
GOBLIN
HOBBIT
KOBOLD
SPRITE
WIZARD

7 letters
BROWNIE
CENTAUR
GREMLIN
GRIFFIN
MERMAID
PEGASUS
SANDMAN
UNICORN

10 letters
HIPPOGRIFF
~~LEPRECHAUN~~

LEPRECHAUN

Illustrated by Carolina Farias

How Ghastly!

1 Remove the lid from a **shoebox**. Paint the inside of the lid with **black paint** and let dry. Paint **three Ping-Pong balls** orange and let dry. Add pumpkin features with **black paint**.

2 Cut out a ghost shape from a piece of **white paper** and glue it inside the lid.

3 Trace a **large thread spool** on the face for the eyes and mouth.

Cut out the circles. Turn the shoebox upside-down, and hold the lid against the bottom. Trace around the three holes.

Cut out the circles.

4 Cut the sides of the shoebox to make legs. Glue the lid to the box bottom, matching up the holes.

To play Drop the three balls onto the lid. Hold the box in your hands, and roll the balls around until you have filled the holes.

Hidden Pictures®
Trick-or-Treaters

sock

crescent moon

pliers

frying pan

candle

broom

cat

baby's bottle

toothbrush

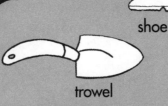
bird

trowel

shoe

book

fire hydrant

pointy hat

81

SCARY SHOPPING

Search these shelves to come up with the answer to this brand-new riddle that's on sale today only. Each clue will help you find one letter. Put the letters in the appropriately numbered spaces. All spaces marked with the same numbers get the same letters. Hurry, because there's a special over in aisle 8!

1. The first letter is in the potatoes.
2. The boxes of soap powder feature this next letter.
3. This letter is on the aisle sign.
4. Pick this letter from the apples.
5. The tentacle is holding this letter.
6. Rivets are holding this letter.
7. Watch out! The bat is flying off with this letter.
8. You'll find this next letter with the cereal.
9. Look for this letter near the peanut butter.
10. This letter is mixed in with the tea bags.

Where do monsters like to shop?

$$\overline{}_{1} \ \overline{}_{2} \quad \overline{}_{3} \quad \overline{}_{4} \ \overline{}_{5} \ \overline{}_{6} \ \overline{}_{7} \ \overline{}_{7} - \overline{}_{8} \ \overline{}_{5} \ \overline{}_{9}$$

$$\overline{}_{7} \ \overline{}_{10} \ \overline{}_{6} \ \overline{}_{5} \ \overline{}_{8} !$$

Illustrated by Terry Kovalcik

83

Maize Maze

Find your way through this tricky cornfield maze from *Enter* to *Exit*. Then try the questions and activities. (By the way, *maize* is another word for corn.)

1 Do you see more bales of hay inside this maze or outside it?

2 As you completed the maze (by the shortest route), did you pass more scarecrows or more bales of hay?

3 Say this five times fast: *One ton of yummy autumn apples.*

4 Find the barrel in this scene.

5 Make at least ten words using letters from the word *cornfield* (such as *cone* or *file*).

1. **What do you call a frankfurter with no meat in it?**

2. What food is never part of a vampire's diet?

3. **What do monsters eat for supper?**

4. How did the monster get in the house?

5. **What's a mummy's favorite game show?**

6. What do polite vampires say to their victims?

7. **What did one Halloween candle say to the other Halloween candle?**

CHUCKLES AND CHILLS

Invisible boy: I just took a test in school. There were twenty questions and I left them all blank.

Invisible mom: So what did you get?

Invisible boy: 100%, of course!

Publisher: I need a spooky story. Do you know anyone who could help me?

Editor: My friend is just the guy you want.

Al: I can't afford a costume this year.

Sal: Don't worry, you can still go to the masquerade party.

Al: As what?

Sal: The Invisible Man.

8. Why did the principal hire the ghost?

9. **Why won't the Invisible Man look in the closet?**

Pam: Did you hear about the new musical group called The Mummies?

Sam: No, what kind of music do they play?

Pam: Wrap!

Publisher: Why him?

Editor: He's a ghost writer.

Illustrated by Terry Sirrell

DR. JEKYLL

A Mighty Meal

Grimbash was a mighty giant who was always hungry. One day he sat down to eat a meal of 30 hamburgers. After Grimbash had eaten 6 of them, his wife, Grizzelda, who also was a giant, came into the kitchen and asked Grimbash to share. Since Grimbash was a nice giant, he evenly split the remaining burgers with his wife. They began eating. After each had eaten 3 burgers, their son, Garrumpus, came in. He was hungry, too. So his parents divided their remaining burgers equally among the three of them. The burgers were quickly eaten, and the giants soon fell fast asleep.

How many burgers did each giant eat?

Illustrated by Michael Austin

Tic Tac Row

Each of these superheroes has something in common with the other two superheroes in the same row. For example, in the first row across all three are flying. Look at the other rows across, down, and diagonally. Can you tell what's alike in each row?

Illustrated by Dave Clegg

Pumpkin Picking

Illustrated by Rocky Fuller

Can you find the hidden objects below?
When you finish, you can color in the rest of the scene.

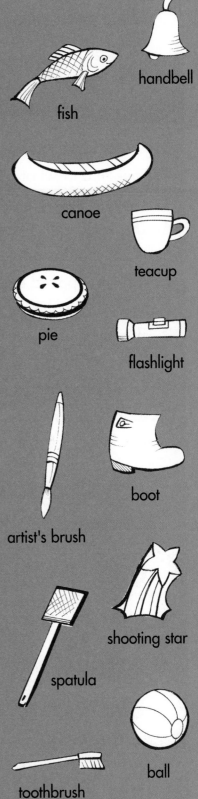

fish

handbell

canoe

teacup

pie

flashlight

artist's brush

boot

spatula

shooting star

toothbrush

ball

Monster Movies

Don't be scared. The answer to this riddle is right in front of your eyes. Read each clue to find out which letters to put in which numbered spaces.

1. The orange monster is clutching this letter.
2. Look in a bowl of popcorn for this letter.
3. The monster on this TV screen has this letter.
4. This letter is in an ice cube.
5. A bat is holding this letter.
6. Look in a potted plant for this letter.
7. Meow! Find the cat to find this letter.
8. This letter is on a hat.
9. Look out a window for this letter.
10. This letter is in a picture frame.
11. Look on a hair bow for this letter.
12. This letter is resting on a pillow.

What do monsters watch movies on?

__ ____ __ __-__ __ __ __ __ __ __ __
2 10 4 7 3 8 6 1 12 11   5 9

Illustrated by Peter Grosshauser

Crafts

You Will Need:

- plastic-foam egg cartons
- hole punch
- yarn
- cardboard egg carton
- paint
- construction paper
- beads
- markers
- thread
- tree branch

Make a Halloween Mobile

These spooky mobiles will bring fleets of ghastly ghosts, batty bats, and "boo-tiful" black cats to your Halloween party. They'll also bring lots of smiles to your guests.

To Make the Ghost Mobile

To make the top, cut the bottom section of a white plastic-foam egg carton in half. Poke a hole in each of the four corner cups. Thread a piece of yarn through each hole and knot the yarn. Join the four pieces of yarn in one knot for a hanger. With a hole punch, make holes to hang the ghosts.

For each ghost, cut five cups from a white plastic-foam egg carton. Poke a hole in the bottom of each cup. Tie a knot at the end of a piece of yarn, and thread a bead onto the yarn. Then thread on one egg cup, then two beads, then another egg cup. Continue in this way until you have put on five cups. Then tie a knot at the top of the ghost's head, and tie the end of the yarn to the top section. Draw on faces with a marker.

To Make the Black Cat Mobile

For the top, cut the lid of a plastic-foam egg carton in half, then cut out a square from the middle of that half. Use the hole punch to make holes in each corner and one hole for each cat. Tie a piece of yarn to each corner hole, and join these four pieces in a knot for a hanger.

For each cat, cut one cup from a cardboard egg carton and trim it into the shape of a cat's head, leaving on pointy ears. Paint the heads black. Glue on paper whiskers and eyes. Poke a hole in the top of each cat's head, and tie a piece of yarn to it. Cover the back of each head with a circle of black paper. Tie each cat to a hole in the top section.

To Make the Bat Mobile

For each bat, cut two cups from a plastic-foam egg carton. Make wings and ears from black paper, and glue them between the cups. Add hole-punch eyes and a mouth. Glue or tape a piece of thread to each bat and tie them to a fallen tree branch. Tie three pieces of yarn to the branch, and gather the pieces in a knot for a hanger.

Get the Joke

There are three jokes about Halloween on the next page. Use the haunted code to fill in the letters and finish the jokes. Then tell them to your friends!

A

B

C

D

E

G

H

I

K

L

M

N

O

R

S

T

U

V

W

What do birds say on Halloween?

"

!"

What kind of dog does Dracula have?

How do you watch movies in a haunted house?

Illustrated by Mike Moran

Moonstruck!

We've hidden 19 words or phrases that contain the letters MOON in this grid. Each time MOON appears in a word, it is replaced by ☾. Look up, down, across, backwards, and diagonally to find the words. Now go search by the light of this moon!

```
        L B Y C C
    ☾ T S E V R A H ☾
  V ☾ F A C E D A F F ☾
    ☾ X T ☾ S ☾ U X G I E
  I S E S C A S W I S S ☾
  O L H T E W ☾ F L A H H T S L
  G N O N F U L L ☾ O L H N C U
  E N T M I E R O B B R K I A N
  E ☾ Y E N O H V L T E K N P A
  V A P O L L O E U H C A A E R
    ☾ F L O W E R E G C R M D
    M O K F E T ☾ I X H N
    C G O ☾ C H I L D N M
    M J R H E L ☾ A D
        X ☾ ☾ D E
```

Hidden Pictures®
Dinnertime Magic

Illustrated by Lynn Adams

hammer

spatula

closed umbrella

dinosaur's head

tea bag

hatchet

shoe

baseball cap

frying pan

mushroom

sailboat

duck

sock

fish

ring

bird

MUSCLE MESSAGE

Exercise can be a scary thing, but it can also be good for you. Match the pictures of each piece of equipment with their corresponding letters to find the coded message. Don't break into a sweat. This should all work out.

S

T

U

V

W

X

Y

Z

I

J

K

L

M

N

O

P

A

B

C

D

E

F

G

H

Illustrated by Jerry Zimmerman

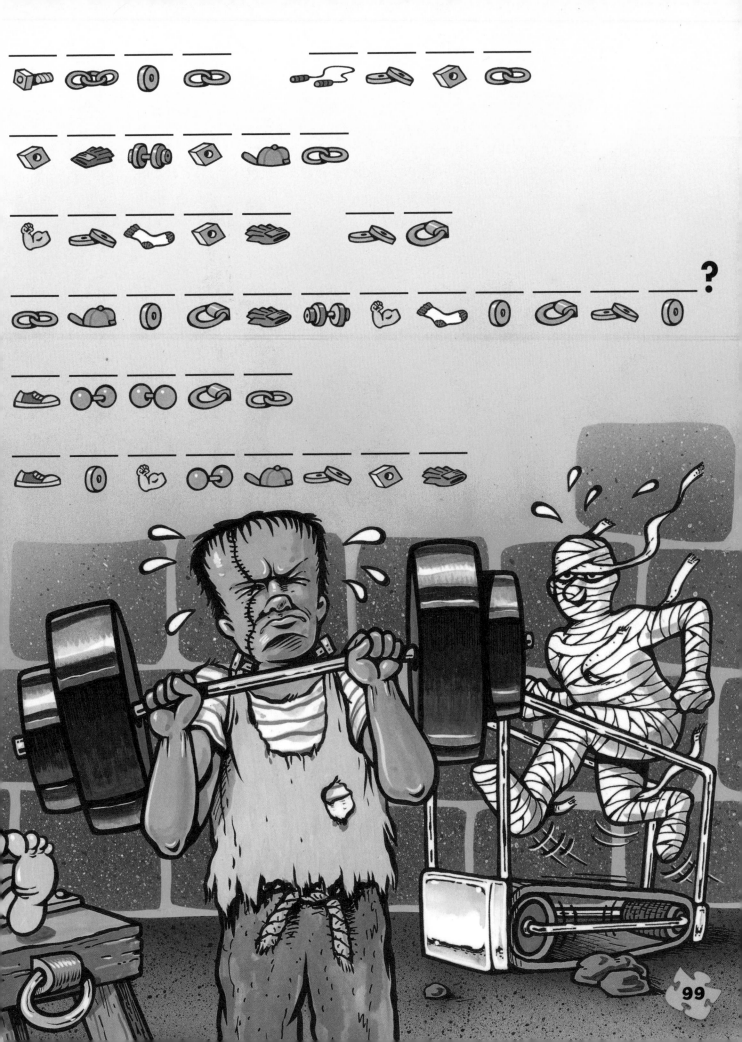

99

Super Savers

Uh-oh! These people need help. Luckily, *Puzzlemania*'s four finest superheroes are on the job! But first they need to get there. Can you help them come to the rescue? Follow the paths to take each superhero to where he or she needs to go.

Tic Tac Row

Each of these monsters has something in common with the other two monsters in the same row. For example, in the top row across, each monster is showing its teeth. Look at the other rows across, down, and diagonally. Can you tell what's alike in each row?

Walk This Way

Don't be afraid! Count Dracula's house may *look* spooky, but he always gives out the best treats, with no tricks. Can you find the shortcut through the pumpkin field to his front door?

finish

start

Illustrated by R. Michael Palan

BATS IN THE BELFRY

Barney is going bats looking up his family tree. Help him find these thirty words that have to do with bats. They're hidden somewhere in the letters on the tree. These words could be anywhere, so look up, down, across, backward, and diagonally in the grid. Once you've found them all, see how many loose bats you can find flying around. Circle BAT as many times as you can find it in this puzzle.

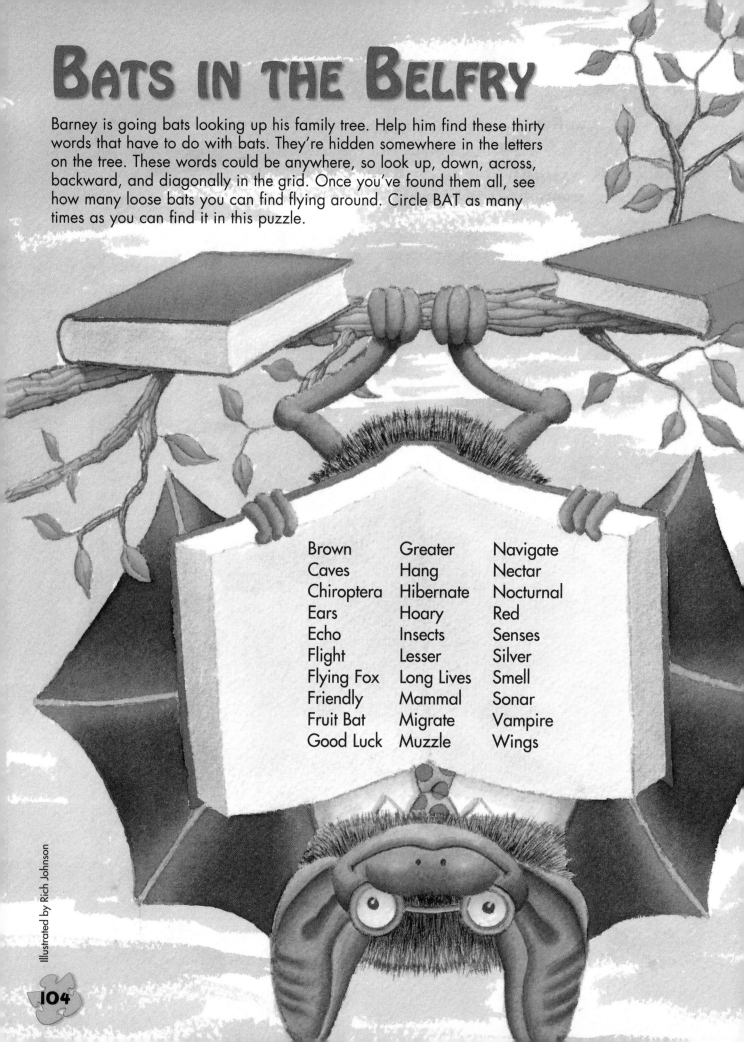

Brown	Greater	Navigate
Caves	Hang	Nectar
Chiroptera	Hibernate	Nocturnal
Ears	Hoary	Red
Echo	Insects	Senses
Flight	Lesser	Silver
Flying Fox	Long Lives	Smell
Friendly	Mammal	Sonar
Fruit Bat	Migrate	Vampire
Good Luck	Muzzle	Wings

```
A N T A B A R E T P O R I H C K
B W I N G S T T R Q T S A F T C
S O S O N A R A L A E N F R A U
T R I Y G R T N B S G K L I B L
C B L I R C S R N A S T I E R D
E T V B E B B E R E T A G N D O
S A E N A A S B V E L B H D E O
N B R T T T A I C A B Z T L R G
I T E S E T L H M B C A Z Y I S
J I S V R G O M T A B A T U P M
B U S P N A A A E T A R G I M E
A R E O R M B N O C T U R N A L
T F L Y I N G F O X S T A B V L
```

105

Illustrated by Dave Klug

There is more than meets the eye on this river trip. Can you find the hidden objects?

car

glove

elephant

artist's brush

slice of pie

banana

slice of orange

pen

eyeglasses

belt

key

pennant

shovel

ladder

ice-cream cone

sneaker

baseball bat

sock

cat

scarf

shoe

cane

mug

slice of pizza

golf club

WORDS ON THE WEB

Use the number pairs to solve the riddle on this page. Move to the right to the first number and then up to the second number. Write the letters you find in the correct spaces.

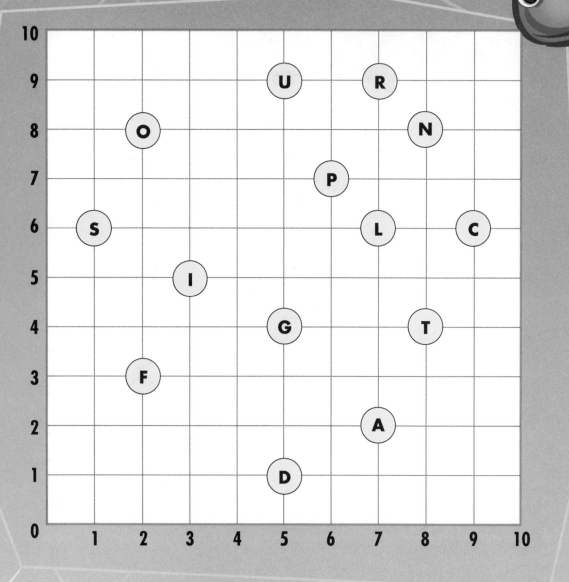

Why did the spider buy a car?

○ ○ ○ ○ ○ ○ ○ ○ ○
1,6 2,8 3,5 8,4 9,6 2,8 5,9 7,6 5,1

○ ○ ○ ○ ○ ○ ○ ○ ○ ○
5,4 2,8 2,3 2,8 7,9 7,2 1,6 6,7 3,5 8,8

Owl Find You

How many owls are hiding in this picture?

strated by Tom Powers

Circle Sense

Each circle in this puzzle represents a group. Use circular logic to figure out what's described

Examples:

1. wild
2. tame

1. Animals that are wild.
2. Animals that are tame.
These two circles are separate because an animal can only be one or the other.

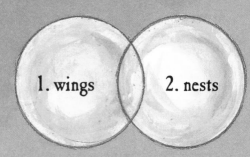

1. wings
2. nests

1. Animals that have wings.
2. Animals that have nests.
These two circles intersect because some animals have wings and also have nests. Those animals would go in the space where the circles overlap. Some animals would go only in the left circle because these animals have wings but do not have nests (like bats). Other animals would go in the right circle because these creatures live in nests but don't have wings (like squirrels).

Now look at the other lists below. Which set of graphs illustrates each list? Write the letter of the correct graph in the box beside the list. Watch the numbers to be sure you have the correct set of graphs.

1. Lead
2. Things that float
3. Things that are alive
□

1. Black objects
2. Crows
3. Things that fly
□

1. Books
2. Nonfiction
3. Fiction
□

1. Roses
2. Red flowers
3. Flowers that bloom in summer
□

1. Band members
2. Flute players
3. First-chair flutists
□

1. Sweet drinks
2. Carbonated drinks
3. Beverages
□

Illustrated by Kit Wray

in each case. Look at the example graphs, called Venn diagrams, first.

A   2.   3.   1.

B   1.   2.   3.

C   1.   2.   3.

D   3.   1.   2.

E   1.   2.   3.

F   1.   2.   3.

October True or False

Some of these facts are true and some are false.
It's up to you to separate the tricks from the treats.

1 October is considered National Car Care Month, National Clock Month, National Computer Learning Month, and National Cosmetology Month.

2 **Father-in-law Day is in October.**

3 Jesse Jackson, Brett Favre, Hillary Clinton, Matt Damon, Bill Gates, and Margaret Thatcher were all born in October.

4 **Jack-o'-lanterns were believed to keep evil spirits away from homes.**

5 Mount Rushmore was completed in October 1941.

6 **The Super Bowl is usually played in October.**

7 The Druids of ancient England believed that October marked the end of the year.

Illustrated by John Manders

Transylvania Polka

Dare to connect these dots and watch what materializes.

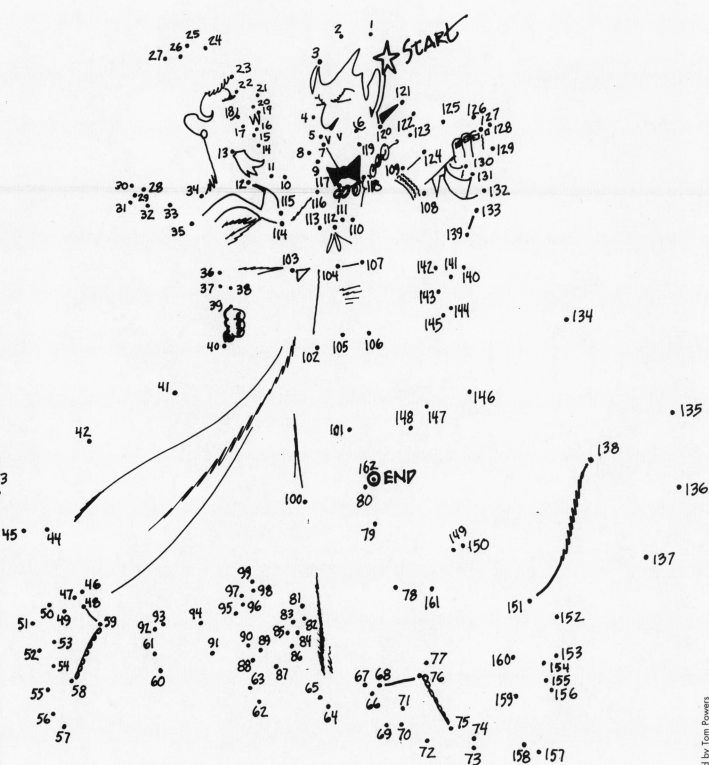

Monster Me

By Eileen Spinelli

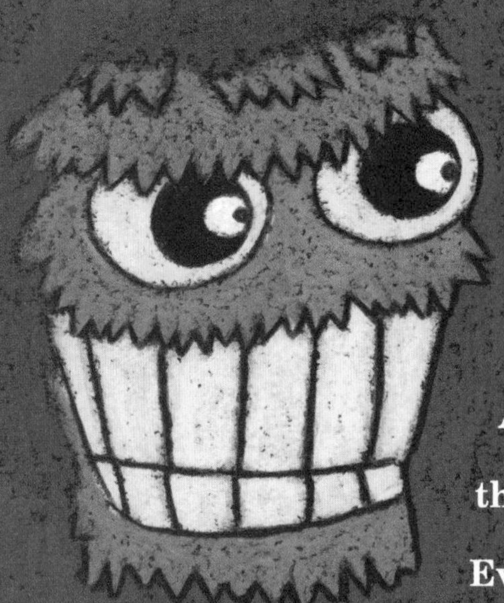

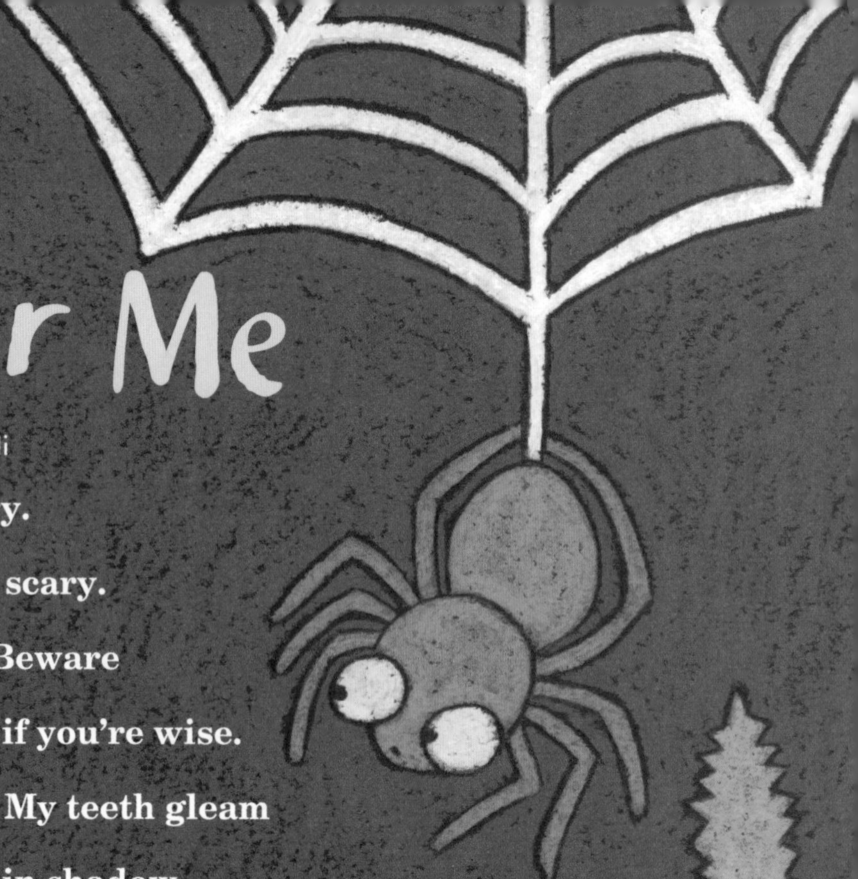

I'm hairy.
I'm scary.
Beware
if you're wise.
My teeth gleam
in shadow
and so do my eyes.
A red spider sees me,
then scuttles away.
Even the bat in the attic
won't stay.
The cat runs for cover.
She's high on the shelf.
I'm so terrifying
I frighten myself!

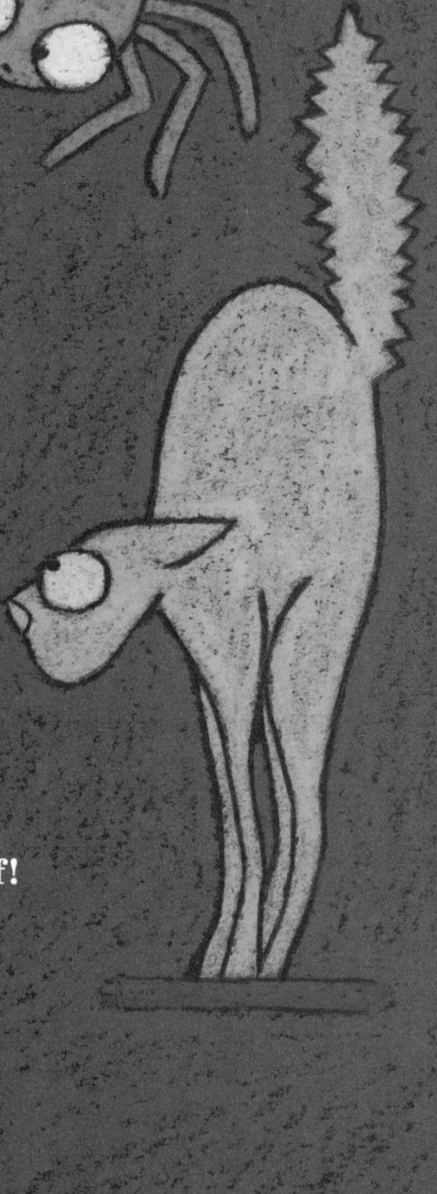

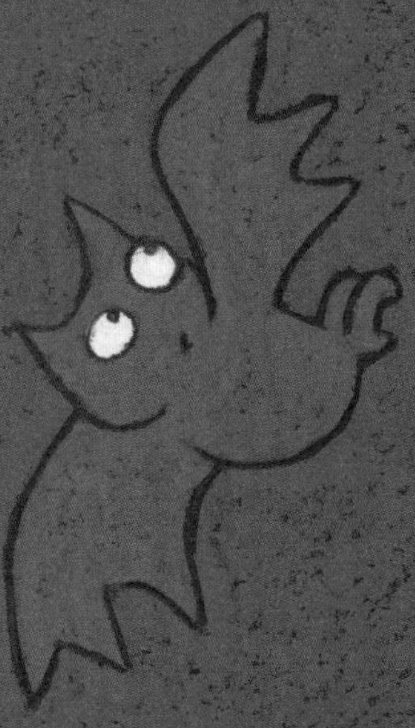

Illustrated by Nancy Coffelt

I'm sticky with cobwebs

and slippy with slime.

And guess where I'm heading

one step at a time—

To your house!

To your house!

I'm now on the stair

that leads to your porch—

Oh, I warned you,

BEWARE!

I rattle your doorknob

and growl when I call.

You open the door, and—

Oh! spoil it all.

For there in the shivering

moonlight it's clear

we're wearing the very same

costume this year!

Hidden Pictures
Trick or Treat!

Can you find the hidden objects below?
When you finish, you can color in the rest of the scene.

spoon

heart

nail

pencil

toothbrush

flashlight

artist's brush

mallet

sock

screwdriver

book

drinking straw

FaLL FaiR FOLLieS

How many silly things can you find in this picture?

Dracula's Spell

Don't get hung up as you unscramble the words below.
Each reveals something that can be worn around the neck.

1 LLORAC _____

2 NICEKET _____

3 WOB ITE _____

4 CELACKEN _____

5 TANDNEP _____

6 FRACS _____

7 SPOTHOSTEEC _____

8 KORCHE _____

9 BANANAND _____

10 IBB _____

11 TOCKLE _____

12 NIACH _____

Illustrated by Jerry Zimmerman

Crafts

Crafty Characters

Invite these creatures to your next Halloween party.

To Make the Basic Character
1. Draw a shape on a plastic-foam tray and cut it out.
2. Cut two notches at the bottom of your character.
3. Cut a circle from a foam tray, then cut it in half.
4. Slide the half circles into the notches.

To Make the Pumpkin

Color your pumpkin shape. Add dark lines down the shape to add dimension.

To Make the Cat

Draw features and legs with colored chalk. Add a collar of glitter.

To Make the Ghosts

Draw features with marker. Outline the ghost in black marker if you wish. Add a pumpkin made of plastic foam or construction paper. Decorate, then glue on a paper or ribbon handle.

You Will Need:
- large and small plastic-foam trays
- colored chalk
- glitter
- permanent markers
- construction paper
- ribbon
- paint and paintbrush

To Make the Witch

Add features with paint, and create a glittering gown and hat.

More Ideas

Cut out dolls or other figures. To make clothes, trace the figures on paper, adding tabs. Decorate the clothes and cut them out.

Hidden Pictures® Pumpkin Decorating

banana

fried egg

comb

wishbone

jar

mushroom

crescent moon

nail

heart

golf club

tack

slice of bread

mug

pitcher

sailboat

musical note

needle

teacup

toothbrush

fishhook

slice of pie

Illustrated by Sally Springer

BeLFry BOUNd

After a long night, Barney is ready to fly home. Can you show him how to get to the belfry without bothering the other bats?

Illustrated by Arthur Friedman

GUESS WHO?

A mystery person can be found in the boxes on the next page.
Two of the characters he created can also be found there.

This person was born in New York City. This person was an essayist, historian, and one of the first of America's great writers. Some of this person's famous works were inspired by stories and legends told by Dutch descendants living in New York. This mystery person, using the pen name Diedrich Knickerbocker, wrote a history of New York. This book brought the word "Knickerbocker" into the English language. This mystery person is buried in Sleepy Hollow Cemetery.

	1	2	3	4	5	6	7	8	9	10	11	12

To solve this puzzle, write the five-letter answer to each clue vertically in the corresponding number column.

When complete, and if done correctly, one character's name will be spelled out across the top row, and a second character's name will be spelled out across the bottom row. The author's last name will appear in the circles, reading from left to right.

1. Plural form of *radius*

2. Sir _____ Newton

3. Horizontal rod or branch that birds stand on

4. A stringed instrument slightly larger than a violin

5. In acting, to make up and perform something on the spur of the moment

6. A chip you cover with cheese

7. Book title: *Around the _____ in Eighty Days*

8. Of or like an ion

9. Not ever

10. Nairobi is the capital of this country

11. Boston airport

12. To wipe out

Illustrated by Judith Hunt

Here Kitty, Kitty

Twenty kinds of cats are hiding in these letters. Can you find them all? They are hidden up, down, across, backwards, and diagonally. If you find **20**, you will end up with a *purr-fect* score!

Word List

- ~~ABYSSINIAN~~
- **BENGAL**
- **BIRMAN**
- **BOMBAY**
- **BURMESE**
- **CHAUSIE**
- **DEVON REX**
- **EXOTIC**
- **KORAT**
- **MAINE COON**
- **MANX**
- **PERSIAN**
- **RAGDOLL**
- **RUSSIAN BLUE**
- **SIAMESE**
- **SIBERIAN**
- **SNOWSHOE**
- **SOMALI**
- **SPHYNX**
- **TURKISH VAN**

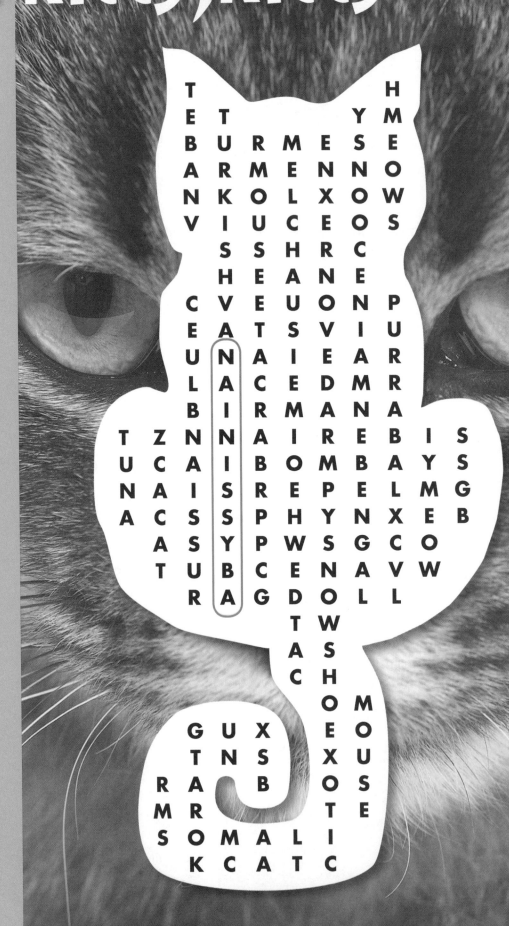

Tic Tac Row

Each of these jack-o'-lanterns has something in common with the other two jack-o'-lanterns in the same row. For example, in the top row across all three are tall pumpkins. Look at the other rows across, down, and diagonally. Can you tell what's alike in each row?

FRIGHT SIGHTS

Oh no! Professor Hink Pink's search to find rhymes has taken him into this haunted house. Now his ghost host is showing off all the scary things that rhyme. How many rhymes can you find in these fright sights?

SQUEAK

R.I.P.
FRED
1608 – 1990

Illustrated by Terry Rogers

Pumpkin Party

Can you find the hidden objects below?
When you finish, you can color in the rest of the scene.

banana

pennant

ring

bracelet

bell

ladle

spatula

wristwatch

spool of thread

sock

feather

ruler

That's the Spirit

How many ghosts can you find haunting this scene?

5 Tic Tac Row

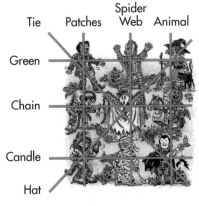

6–7 Match-o'-Lanterns

8–9 Bat-ting Order

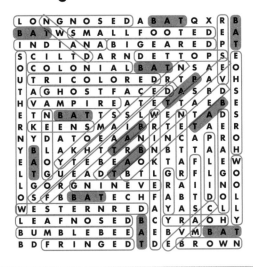

10–11 Monster Maze

What is a werewolf's favorite book?
HAIRY POTTER

12 Haunted House

14–15 Boo!

Where do monsters go to water ski?
LAKE EERIE

How do you mend a broken jack-o'-lantern?
WITH A PUMPKIN PATCH

What is a ghost's favorite party game?
HIDE-AND-GO-SHRIEK

Why don't mummies take vacations?
THEY DON'T WANT TO RELAX AND UNWIND.

Answers

16–17 Hidden in the Pumpkin Patch

18 Spooky Search

19 Box Out!

M 8	T 13	Y 40	N 24	H 17	A 12
O 15	M 16	C 33	E 20	C 18	A 30
L 32	E 25	F 48	T 36	L 10	O 64
R 45	F 28	D 3	R 66	A 26	Y 42
Z 56	E 21	B 38	B 72	T 80	W 54
E 22	K 39	N 51	H 6	T 44	S 27

What do magical creatures learn in school?
THE ELF-ABET

20–21 Mansion of Mystery

If you've followed the directions correctly, you've found
COMIC BOOKS.

25 Up All Night

26 Wendy Witch's Stew

27 A Total Hoot

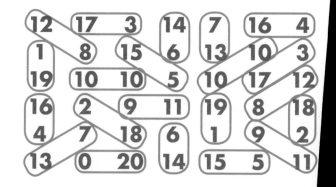

29 Who's There?

1. Knock knock. Who's there?
Doris. Doris who?
Doris locked, that's why I had to knock.

2. Knock knock. Who's there?
Sadie. Sadie who?
Sadie magic words and I'll tell you.

3. Knock knock. Who's there?
Noah. Noah who?
Noah good place to find more jokes?

30–31 Castle Calculation

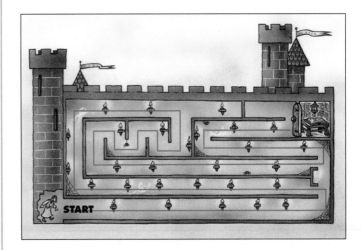

32 Open House

33 Scrambled Bugs

ANT	BEETLE
MOTH	BEDBUG
FLEA	CRICKET
WASP	MOSQUITO
TICK	DRAGONFLY
GNAT	GRASSHOPPER

Where does a spider keep its photos?
ON ITS WEB SITE

34–35 Monster Mash

Why do grave diggers make excellent storytellers?
BECAUSE THEY DIG UP GOOD PLOTS

36–37 Laboratory Labyrinth

135

Answers

39 Tic Tac Row

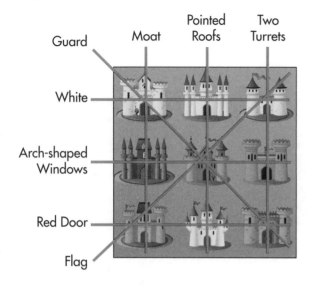

Guard · Moat · Pointed Roofs · Two Turrets

White

Arch-shaped Windows

Red Door

Flag

44–45 Party Time

47 Spooky Sale

42 Haunted Logic

Trevor: robot, raisins
Rachel: ghost, chocolate bars
Eli: baseball player, licorice
Annie: dragon, gum
Troy: tiger, taffy

46 Going Batty

48–49 Puzzling Pirates

Blackbeard: Hawaii, bag, silver, *Jolly Roger*
Orangebeard: Tahiti, metal box, baseball cards, *Ocean Queen*
Whitebeard: Haiti, chest, gold, *Leaking Lena*
Purplebeard: Backyard, jar, jewels, *Smiling Sea Gull*
Super Challenge: Blackbeard was a real pir

O Candy Counter

```
C A R A M E L              J
    I            C A N D Y C A N E
    C A N D Y C A N E      L
    T        H            L
        L I C O R I C E   Y
    L        O           B
    O   T R U F F L E     E
    L   U        A       A
    L   D        T A F F Y N
    I   G        B
    P   E        A
    O   G        B
    P E A N U T B R I T T L E
        U
        M
```

at crop does a farmer with a sweet tooth grow?

CANDY CORN

51 Tic Tac Row

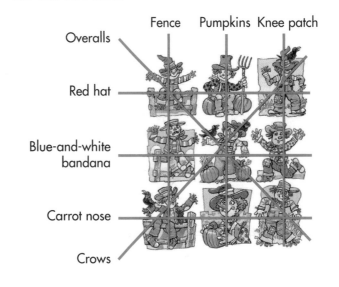

Fence   Pumpkins   Knee patch

Overalls

Red hat

Blue-and-white bandana

Carrot nose

Crows

2–53 A Squeaky House

54 Minus Maze

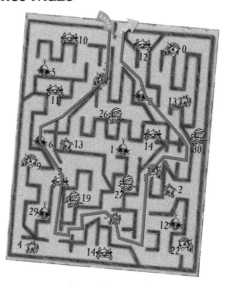

6–57 Monster Party

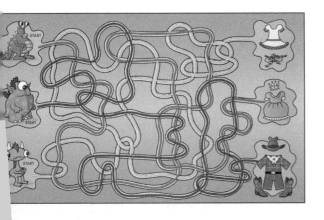

58–59 Halloween Parade

Answers

60 Snooperstition

GOOD LUCK

fingers crossed
horseshoe
salt over shoulder
four-leaf clover
wishbone

BAD LUCK

cracked mirror
Friday the 13th
walk under the ladder
number 13
black cat
stepping on a crack
umbrella open indoors

62–63 Leaves and Bounds

64–65 Whose Home?

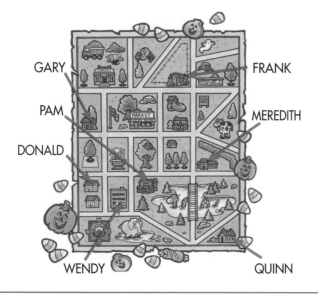

66 Mummy Maze

68 Carving Jack-o'-Lanterns

70–71 Adventures in the Night

Answers

2–73 Party Search

74 Don't Be Afraid...

5 Liquid Fun

A gallon will fill a quart 4 times.
A gallon will fill a pint 8 times.
A pint will fill a cup 2 times.
A quart will fill a pint 2 times.
A gallon will fill a cup 16 times.

76–77 Trick or Treat?

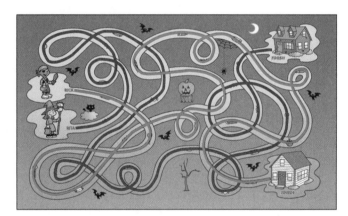

Rick: 14, Rita: 15. Rita collected more candy.

8–79 Imagine That!

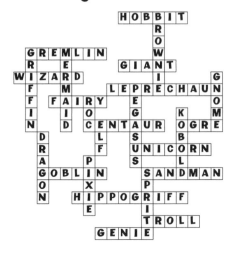

81 Trick-or-Treaters

139

Answers

82–83 Scary Shopping

Where do monsters like to shop?
IN A GROSS-ERY STORE!

84 Maize Maze

1. Outside (14)
2. More bales
4. Under the banjo player

85 Chuckles and Chillls

1. A Hollow-weeny
2. Steaks
3. Ghoul-ash and grave-y
4. With a skeleton key
5. Name That Tomb
6. "Fangs a lot!"
7. "You look wicked tonight."
8. To give his school more spirit
9. Because he can never find anything
   to wear!

86 A Mighty Meal

Grimbash—15
Grizzelda—9
Garrumpus—6

87 Tic Tac Row

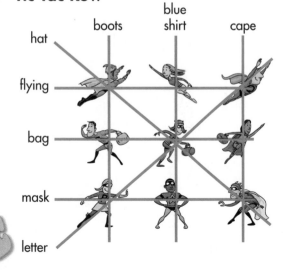

88–89 Pumpkin Picking

O–9I Monster Movies

What do monsters watch movies on?
A BIG-SCREAM TV

94–95 Get the Joke

What do birds say on Halloween?
"TRICK OR TWEET!"

What kind of dog does Dracula have?
A BLOODHOUND

How do you watch movies in a
haunted house?
ON A BIG-SCREAM TV

6 Moonstruck!

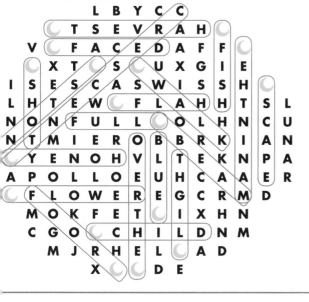

97 Dinnertime Magic

8–99 Muscle Message

WHAT DIET EXPERT LIVES IN
TRANSYLVANIA?

COUNT CALORIES

100–10I Super Savers

Answers

102 Tic Tac Row

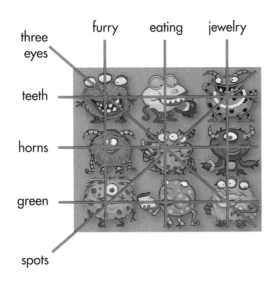

three eyes — teeth — horns — green — spots

furry — eating — jewelry

103 Walk This Way

104–105 Bats in the Belfry

There are twenty-one BATs flying loose.

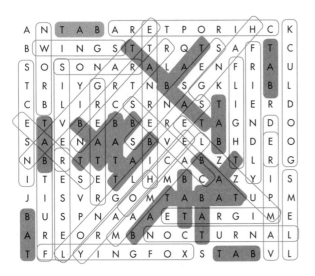

106–107 Hidden on the River

108 Words on the Web

Why did the spider buy a car?
SO IT COULD GO FOR A SPIN

IIO–III Circle Sense

A. (2)(3) (1)
1. Lead
2. Things that float
3. Things that are alive

B.
1
2
3
1. Band members
2. Flute players
3. First-chair flutists

C. (1)(2) 3
1. Black objects
2. Crows
3. Things that fly

D.
3
(1)(2)
1. Sweet drinks
2. Carbonated drinks
3. Beverages

E.
1   2
3
1. Roses
2. Red flowers
3. Flowers that bloom in summer

F.
1
(2 3)
1. Books
2. Nonfiction
3. Fiction

Transylvania Polka

Dracula's Spell

COLLAR
NECKTIE
BOW TIE
NECKLACE
PENDANT
SCARF

7. STETHOSCOPE
8. CHOKER
9. BANDANNA
10. BIB
11. LOCKET
12. CHAIN

II2 October True or False

Number 2 and number 6 are incorrect.

Mother-in-law Day is in October, and the Super Bowl is usually played in January.

II6–II7 Trick or Treat!

I22 Pumpkin Decorating

Answers

123 Belfry Bound

124–125 Guess Who?

	1	2	3	4	5	6	7	8	9	10	11	12
	R	I	P	(V)	A	N	W	(I)	N	K	L	E
	A	S	E	I	D	A	O	O	E	E	O	R
	D	A	(R)	O	L	C	R	N	V	(N)	(G)	A
	(I)	A	C	L	I	H	L	I	E	Y	A	S
	I	C	H	A	B	O	D	C	R	A	N	E

Rip Van Winkle and **Ichabod Crane** are two characters created by Washington **Irving**.

126 Here Kitty, Kitty

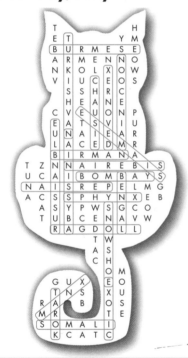

127 Tic Tac Row

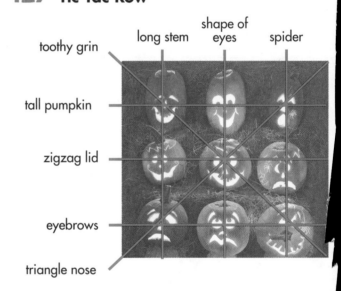

toothy grin · long stem · shape of eyes · spider · tall pumpkin · zigzag lid · eyebrows · triangle nose

130–131 Pumpkin Party

128–129 Fright Sights

The rhymes shown by the ghost host include:

frightening lightning
squeaker sneaker
pants dance
book hook
fat bat
scary canary
rich witch
hobblin' goblin

dead Fred
scare chair
bone phone
mummy tummy
moose noose
lime slime
black crack

144